The
Success Manual
For
Small Businesses

Copyright

Dedication

This book is dedicated to the men and women who work super hard every day to run their business and provide valuable products and services to people. It is dedicated to small business owners everywhere.

Index

Preface

The purpose of this book is to wake you up, to open your eyes and to turn your business upside down. After reading this, I believe you would no longer see your business, your products & services, your employees and your customers in the way that you currently do.

You'd start understanding why big successful businesses are doing what they're doing. You would start seeing all your past business experiences, your current situation and everything that happens in your business from now on in a new light. The market, economic, competition and government problems that previously bothered you and still bother others will disappear.

The strategies mentioned in this book have the power to increase your business success beyond your wildest dreams. Business is one of the most important yet misunderstood topics in the world, therefore you need to start by understanding where your business currently stand, because it's unlikely that you already know, otherwise you won't be here reading this book.

EVALUATE WHERE YOU ARE

Before you can move forward you must know where you already stand and have a clear destination in mind that you need to move towards.

When someone doesn't feel well and visit a doctor, they first need to tell the doctor what's wrong with them and only then the doctor can begin curing them.

Same principle applies in the business world too.

People try to cure their business problem without even knowing what the problem is and where it is coming from.

The point is, most small businesses don't know what the reason behind their success is or what the reason behind their lack of success is?

Below you'll find 20 questions that if you answer would help you understand the current position of your business. After answering these questions you would be able to come up with specific strategies to grow your business:

1. Why I started my business in the first place? (What caused or motivated me?)
2. How did my initial (first few) customers found my business?

3. Why did my initial customers bought from me?
4. What marketing method brings the maximum number of customers to me?
5. What percentage of my customers come from that (above mentioned) marketing method?
6. How much money on average do I spend on marketing to get one new customer?
7. What are all the marketing methods I use to promote my business? (TV ads, magazine ads, online marketing etc.)
8. Where do my customers come from? (demographically)
9. Do I earn more money from business with new customers or from repeated business with regular customers?
10.   What is my business? Define completely (What you sell, how you sell and whom you sell to?)
11. What problem does my product or service solves?
12. How long on average does a customer stays with me? (keeps doing business with me)
13. How much money on average does a customer spends with me over one transaction?
14. What is the most common complaint customers have with my products or service?
15. What benefits do people get by buying from me instead of my competitors?
16. Who is my biggest competitor and what does he/she offer that I don't?
17. Why my competitor's customers buy from him instead of me?
18. Do my customers only and always buy from me or do they keep switching between me and competitors?
19. Is there any free source that's brining me customers? (Word-of-mouth, great location etc.)
20. Can I contact and get back the customers who previously did business with me but stopped for some reason?

When you answer these questions you would immediately find few flaws in your business and would come up with multiple ways to fix them.

By evaluating where you currently stand you'd be able to apply the strategies mentioned in this book more easily, quickly and effectively.

FIVE
STRATEGIES

ONE: DON'T SELL, SERVE

"A satisfied customer is the best business strategy of all." – Michael LeBoeuf

Why is it that some people and businesses achieve so much more success than others?

It's not because people running those businesses are smarter than everybody else. It's not because those businesses have technical, manufacturing or labour advantages that others do not possess. And it's definitely not because of luck.

So what is it that makes some people so much more successful than others?

The difference is in the way they think about their customers and how they approach and treat them.

They don't try to sell customer a product or service just so they can make the largest possible one time profit from them. Instead, they understand the exact needs and desires of the customer and lead them to the fulfilment of those desires in the best possible manner.

For example, a person who goes to a store to buy a camera doesn't actually want the camera, they want high quality pictures which they can preserve and see whenever they want to.

Similarly, a person who buys a car doesn't want the object car, he wants a comfortable and convenient way of traveling wherever he wants to.

Highly successful businesses, understand such hidden needs of their customers and they make 'getting the customer to his desired end result' their objective, not just selling a one-time product.

Instead of thinking of your customer as a person whom you need to extract money from, think of him as a dear friend. Just by doing this you'll build a long term and highly profitable relationship with him.

This one simple change in your thinking would increase your business more than all the other success strategies in the world combined.

People would wait in line to do business with you. Your competitor's customers would literally ditch them and spend their money with you. Your customers would not only be your clients but they'd become your lifelong friends.

Understand The Real Needs

The only thing that you need to do to successfully implement this strategy in your business is to move your focus from yourself or your business to your customers. It means you should focus on what your customers want more than what you want.

It's weird to see how companies and salesmen do and say whatever it takes to sell a single product instead of understanding what the customer really wants.

They sell their products to the customer even if they know that their products are not going to solve the customer's real problem. They use all kind of lies and selling techniques and try to persuade the customer into buying from them.

This sometimes gets them the initial sale but takes the customer away from them. That person is not going to return to their store when he needs something else neither is he going to recommend that store to any of his friends.

Serve

Instead of selling to your customers, start serving them. This means you don't sell them a product or service just so you can make a large one-time profit. You try to understand exactly what they want even if they themselves are unsure of it and then you lead them to getting that result. This way you might not make the largest initial sale but you do own the person and they remains your customer for life.

No matter what business or industry you're in, if you focus on solving problem and serving instead of instant selling, you'll build a lot of lifelong customers, clients and friends and you'll receive rewards in ways you can't even imagine.

Love People Not Products

As a business owner you must immensely believe in your products and services and try to make them as good as possible but you shouldn't fall in love with them instead you should fall in love with your customers.

Falling in love means you must take responsibility for their needs. You must put your customer's needs before yours. Instead of asking yourself "what should I say to sell?" ask yourself, "What result does the customer wants and what do I have or what can I give that would help the customer get that result?"

Successful selling has nothing to do with persuasion or trick and has everything to do with how you serve and treat your customers.

Change the way you talk to your customers. How do you behave when you're talking to a dear friend or someone you care about? Behave in the same way with your customers too.

Genuinely respect the importance of their time and comfort. Never keep them waiting for too long. Make your store or office a comfortable place for them. Offer them water or other beverages and have comfortable and clean sitting arrangement for them etc.

Follow up after the sale to make sure your product or service is delivered, installed and working properly and solve any problem or questions that your customers have regarding it.

Remember your customers are humans with emotions and needs not an ATM machine or a checkbook. Their satisfaction and happiness is what you success depends on.

Remember They're Humans

Whether you're selling to individuals or a big corporation, always remember that eventually whom you're dealing with are human beings and as such they'll always have some needs and problems.

It's up to you to understand what their needs and problems are and then sell them the solution to that. Successful businesses not just sell products but solve problems.

Don't be in a business just for the purpose of making money. Do business for solving problems and making life of other people better and easier.

Whatever business you're in, you're always solving some kind of problems and fulfilling some needs. Make the act of solving that problem your purpose in life not just earning money.

The best thing about this strategy is that it works in every business and in every job irrelevant of their industry, size or locality. You always have to do the same things:

Understand the end result your customer wants,
Lead them into getting that result in the best possible way and
Treat them as humans not an ATM machine

Things To Remember

Extremely successful businesses don't just try to make a one-time sale they try solve their customer's problems.

Treat your customers as you would treat a dear friend or relative.

Focus more on what your customers want instead of what you want.

Take responsibility for the fulfilment of your customer's need.

Your success depends on your customer's success.

TWO: BE DIFFERENT

"If you don't drive your business, you will be driven out of business"
– B. C. Forbes

How could you make people do business with you instead of your competitors? Especially if you're in an industry with huge competition?

The solution is simple, give your customers an advantage, a benefit or a reward that none of your competitors are offering.

Offering something different, something unique and something that no one else is offering would give people a big reason to choose you over others.

It will increase the number of customers you attract and at the same time would make them keep coming back to do business with you again and again.

This benefit/reward would be your "Unique Selling Proposition (USP)". It will make your business different than the business of your competitors.

Some USP examples are:

FedEx: When it absolutely, positively have to be there

Dominos: Delivered in 30 minutes or it's free

Amazon: 24 hour delivery

Creating Your Usp

Every industry and every company has a different USP. Look at some ads, newspapers, banners etc. and notice what USPs different businesses are using. This would help you create your own USP.

Some things you can build your USP about include:

Lower price
Better quality
Faster delivery
Installation help
24 hour customer service
Easy returns
Longer warranty
Satisfaction or money back guarantee
Vast collection
Etc.

There are unlimited numbers of things you can build your USP about although the bigger the problem your USP solves the better it performs.

To get ideas for creating a USP:

First of all, write down on a paper all the benefits and advantages you offer to your customers.

Then, write down all the advantages that your competitors offer that you don't.

Then think about how you can improve upon the benefits that your competitor is offering to the customers.

Also, create a list of all the businesses that you're a customer of.

Think of why you prefer to do business with them instead of any of their competitor? What benefit do they offer to you over their competition?

See if you can apply those same benefits in your business as your USP?

It's important that you fulfil the promise that you've made in your USP. If you can't deliver what you said, you'll end up losing customers instead of gaining. If you're not sure you can fulfil your USP than change it to something that you're sure you can fulfil.

If your USP is that you deliver products anywhere in US within 24 hours of the order than by all means do it. Failure to fulfil your promise would result in a bad reputation and loss in business.

Majority of the businesses doesn't have any USP, they just have a "me too" business. They give people no particular reason for buying from them instead of their competitors.

Few businesses actually have a USP and those few businesses perform better than all of their competitors combined.

You don't always have to come up with a unique benefit or service as a USP, there could be something good that you're already doing in your business that could be used as your USP.

For example: If you run a restaurant and you have your own small farm where you grow fresh stuff for your restaurant. You can use this as your USP telling people that your food is made with fresh & organic items.

Presenting Your USP

Write a one paragraph statement stating your USP. Don't try to compress it in the beginning it's fine to use two or more paragraphs. After completely writing the full USP, remove all the unnecessary words and information from the paragraphs and narrow it down to a small and specific statement clearly presenting the benefit of your USP.

Use this clear statement in every marketing and advertising campaign that you use for your business. Make all the people that work for your business especially salesmen to use this USP every time they deal with potential customers.

Make sure your USP statement is present in all your ads. For example (the restaurant and fresh food example):

We Always Prepare Your Food With
Fresh & Organic Vegetables
Grown In Our Own Farm

Or…

**Most Restaurants Use Frozen And Stale
Raw Materials To Prepare Your Food**

**We Make Food With Fresh & Organic Raw Materials Grown In Our
Own Farm Under Careful Supervision**

Mention your USP in every form of marketing you use including
phone sales and face-to-face selling. Whenever you or someone from
your staff is dealing with a customer make sure you explain the USP
to them clearly.

You must always display to the customer that your USP is more
beneficial to them then your competitors USP (if they even have one).

If you have previously successfully delivered the benefit of your USP
to other customers then use those stories as examples of how you
always honestly fulfil your USP.

Tons of businesses makes up most of their profit from repeated or
backend sales and for those businesses it's extremely important that
their USP stays in the minds of their customers even after the initial
sale, so that when it's time to buy again the customer remembers and
visit them.

To make your customers remember you after the sale, you'll need to
follow up immediately after the sale. Either call, write or visit them
and ask about the performance of your product while doing this repeat
your USP multiple times and remind the customer how your USP
helped them.

You can also create occasional special one-time offers (OTO) as your USP, for example:

Normal USP: Buy one get one free
Special OTO USP: Buy one get two free

Normal USP: 2 year extended warranty
Special OTO USP: 5 year extended warranty

Things To Remember

Offering something unique, something different that no one else is offering would make people do business with your instead of others.

This is known as USP (Unique Selling Proposition)

USP makes your business unique and more valuable than your competitors and thus gives you an edge in the market.

Always, fulfil the promise that you make in your USP

Include your USP in all your marketing campaigns.

THREE: INCREASE THE SIZE OF EVERY SALE

"There is only one boss. The customer. And he can fire everybody in the company from the chairman on down, simply by spending his money somewhere else." – Sam Walton

Whenever someone buys something from you it is because they trust and respect you and they believe that you would get them the result they need. They think of you as a trusted person who has knowledge regarding what they want. Otherwise they won't be standing at your office or your store offering their money to you. But are you giving them everything that you have to offer that would bring them closer to their desired result?

Most businesses limit their own business by not offering the customers all the products they could be offering and they're not even aware of this.

Think about this – is there anything else that your customers could buy from you beside the basic product that would help them with the end result that they're after? If the answer is yes then aren't you limiting your own business by not offering them that thing?

What you're about to learn will help you give more benefits to your customers and at the same time put more instant cash into your pocket.

The strategy is to give your customers the option of buying other things related to their basic purchase that together makes the product better and complete for them. For example: The option of buying screen glass and back cover after buying the phone.

As you've learnt by now that people don't buy products or services they buy end result. For example; a person buying camera actually needs the end result of having high quality beautiful pictures not the camera itself.

Therefore, if you understand the end result that the customer wants, you can figure out what other products they would need to achieve that end result and you can sell them those products.

This one strategy would increase your instant income (as you'd sell more products right on the spot), increase your business (as that customer would keep coming back and buying from your again and again) and would increase your number of customers (as the customer would refer your business to other people).

This strategy could be seen working in automobile industry. When you buy a car the company immediately try to sell you related items such as; stereo system, insurance, sun roof etc.

They understand you don't just want a car but want a great travel experience and they know what else you'd need to make your experience great.

Don't think of this technique as a way to manipulate customers into buying multiple things from you instead think of it as a way to give your customers all the things they need in order to attain their desired end result.

This technique is highly beneficial for the customers as well, they get everything they need at one stop and don't have to go to different places and buy every item separately.

Related Product "ADD-ON"

Offer people every other product that is required along with the basic product that they've bought from you. For example;

Sell antivirus, headphones, pen-drives, printers, installation service etc. along with laptop and desktop.

Do hotel bookings, cab bookings etc. along with flight bookings.

The customer might think he only needs the basic product when he came to your office or store but it's your responsibility to understand what he intend to use the product for and whether or not the basic product alone can get him the result he's after?

If it can't, then offer him the related products that he actually would require for the attainment of his outcome.

Creating Your "ADD-ON"

Step #1: Write down on a paper the three best-selling items of your store.

Step #2: Take a single item and find out what end result are customers looking for when they purchase that item.

Step #3: Think about what other products or services you can provide along with that item that would bring the customer closer to the end result they want.

Put yourself in your customer's shoes and think from their point of view, what other item or service do they need in order to achieve their desired end result?

Step #4: Notice what your customers do before they purchase your goods or services. For example; if you have a teaching business regarding some topic then you should also sell the tools required to perform the activity that you've just taught them.

Step #5: Notice what your customers do after buying things from you, how they carry it to their house or wherever they need it, how they install it and take care of it and can you provide these services to them for a fee?

Step #6: Notice what people buy before and after they purchase your product and if those items relate with your product then start selling them at your store.

Remove the headache for your customer of having to go to multiple different places and indulge in multiple different transactions and deal with multiple different people.

Volume ADD-ON

Your customers would buy more than they usually do if you give them a better deal on a long term option.

There are many products that need to be renewed regularly such as; soaps, deodorants, food items like butter etc. and they can all be packed in larger packages and offered together at lower rate.

Ask yourself, in your business is it possible to give customers a larger unit of your product. For example, a monthly or yearly supply or a family package etc.

Reduce the price as you increase the unit of items. For example; four units for the price of three, or buy three and get one free.

This makes you more money initially and also gives the customers a discount that he wouldn't get by buying individually.

Previously Disneyland sold individual tickets per ride to the visitors. They soon realized that if they sell packages including multiple rides then they can charge more money and have more sales as well.

They now sell family plans and season ticket plans. This gives families the advantage of enjoying multiple rides for lower rate per ride and at the same time makes more money to Disneyland.

Subscription ADD-ON

Another type of add-on is where you increase the time period instead of volume. For example, one year or two-year subscription of magazine.

In this case you reduce the price of the subscription as you increase the time period. Example, monthly subscription for $20 per month, yearly subscription for $200 i.e. $16.66 per month and so on.

The subscription add-on can be used with every service and product that requires continuous renewal like;

Newspaper or magazine subscription
Dry cleaning service
Car wash service
Pest control service
Medical check-up
Medication and supplements
Gym membership. Etc.

With subscription add-on you can convert one-time buyers into your regular customers as they won't leave after the first sale but would stay with you till their subscription ends.

Also, statistically majority of the customers renew their subscription with the same vendor after it's over instead of choosing a different vendor.

Things To Remember

Customer doesn't want a product, they want an end result which in most cases requires having multiple products and selling all those products together would increase your initial revenue and make it easy for customer to get the end result.

Think from your customer's point of view, what else would they need along with your product that together would help them get their desired end result?

Related product add-on: Selling all the products that are needed together in the attainment of an end result

Volume add-on: Increasing the volume of products and making a big package while at the same time reducing the price per unit.

Subscription add-on: Giving people the option of buying the product or service for long term for lower price.

FOUR: MAKE IT SAFE

"Sales are contingent upon the attitude of the salesman - not the attitude of the prospect." – W. Clement Stone

Suppose, you want to buy something and you've found two vendors selling that thing. The product both of the vendors are selling is similar in almost every manner but…

…the first vendor is giving you a take it or leave deal of $200 for that product. The second vendor however is selling the product for $250 but he's allowing you to take the product to your house use it for one week and only pay if your liked it.

Which vendor are you going to buy from?

There's no doubt that almost every person is going to buy from the second vendor. Similarly, in your business if you give people a risk-free deal there's no doubt that everyone is going to buy from you instead of your competitors.

The biggest obstacle in buying is fear. The fear of ending up buying a useless product and thus wasting money. When you take this fear away you make it easier for the customer to take action.

You must take the risk in every transaction. Tell your customers that if they're unsatisfied with your product or service, you would give them a full refund or give them a new product for free or re-do the job for no additional charge.

Most of the businesses actually do have some form of risk reversal offer but they never display it in their ads or use it in their marketing strategies. They unconsciously hide it from their customers.

Your message should be clearly displayed and stated in all your advertising and marketing campaigns. You must make sure that everyone who knows about your business knows that have a risk reversal offer.

Creating Your Offer

The risk reversal offer is where you guarantee the total and full satisfaction of the customer and take fear completely out of the transaction. This makes people do business with your instead of your competitors.

Ask yourself; what do your customers want from your product or service? What end result are they after when they buy that product or service? Promise them that they will get that end result or you'd give them their full money back.

There are cases where risk reversal offers don't make any difference it's mostly because the competitors also offer the same risk reversal deal.

In such situations you need to offer greater benefits than simply refunding the money. You need to have something more than just a risk free offer.

You do this by making the promise of not only refunding their money if they're unsatisfied but to also give them some reward for putting their trust in you.

Tell your customers that if for whatever reason they are not happy with your product or service, you will give them a complete refund and at the same time you will also give them compensation.

For instance suppose you sell Green Tea for losing weight. Here's how you can present your risk-free offer;

"If (product name) doesn't make you lose 5 pounds in the next 20 days then not only will I give you a complete refund but (compensation).

Here are some examples of incentives you can offer as compensation;

I will personally pay you $100 extra for trying (product name).

I will buy you one month supply of green tea from the company of your choosing.

I will pay you (twice the prize of your product).

If your product is actually good, you'd hardly ever need to provide the incentive but just having this offer would give your business a big advantage over the competition.

Before deciding on any compensation offer, try offering different incentives for a fixed period of time and see which incentive brings the most sales to you.

A study done by automobile companies show that the biggest reason people don't buy something is because they are afraid to look bad in front of their peers and thus try to avoid making a mistake.

When you have a strong risk reversal offer, you eliminate people's fear of making a mistake and looking stupid. They understand that they don't lose anything even if product doesn't perform well.

Specific Guarantee

When you start offering a clear and specific risk reversal guarantee, your sales would begin to increase almost immediately.

The more specific the guarantee is the better it performs. For example:

Unspecific guarantee: "Satisfaction Guaranteed"

Specific guarantee: "If within 2 weeks you didn't feel like your face looks more youthful and radiant we will give an immediate 100% refund. No questions asked and no hard feelings"

Having specific guarantees always increases the sales. There's no promise on how much of the sales would increase, it could increase by 50% or even by 500% it depends on multiple factors like; your product, the guarantee you offer and what your competitors are offering, but they will increase for sure.

Also, by having a specific and powerful guarantee you display your trust in your product or service. People can see that you believe in yourself and this make them believe in you too.

By not having the risk of losing anything, people feel comfortable in taking action and buying. And if your product and service actually performs as you say, people would come and buy from you again and again plus they'll refer you to their friends as well.

That being said, you must stand behind what you promise and deliver it perfectly when you're supposed to. If someone is dissatisfied with your product and your offer says that you give 100% refund, then you must give it to that person.

If you don't fulfil the promise of refund or compensation that you offer, you'll end up losing customers and reputation plus since your offer is in written proof you could even end up facing legal problems.

Make It More Powerful

How to make your risk reversal offers more powerful?

Answer; Increase their time period. If you previously or your competitor offers 30 day money back guarantee you could start offering 45 days or 60 days money back guarantee.

Double time period could easily double the effectiveness of the offer. The more clearly you promise people the result they must get from your product or service, the more they want to buy it.

The more specific and detailed the guarantee is, the more powerful it becomes. Which of the following guarantees do you think is more powerful?

First: "30 days money back guarantee"

Second: "If in the next 30 days *(product)* doesn't *(its function)* and you're unsatisfied, just visit us or send us an email at *(email address)* and we'll send your every penny back immediately. No questions asked and no hard feelings."

Do you notice how powerful the guarantee becomes when you make it more clear, detailed and specific? By using such specific guarantees you would almost instantly start attracting more customers to your business.

When you eliminate the fear of losing and wasting money from your business, people will begin to buy from you instantly, buy more volume of products and buy more often.

By using risk reversal offer in your business, you are non-verbally telling your customers that no matter what, they'll never end up wasting their money by doing business with you.

You'll begin to start attracting people who were previously only mildly interested in your products or service and you will begin to start attracting people who were previously confused between choosing you or your competitors.

You must display your clear, specific risk reversal offer in all your marketing and advertising campaigns. You and everyone who works for you must mention this offer whenever dealing with a potential customer.

Make your risk reversal offer more powerful than your competitors by increasing the time period, increasing the compensation incentive or just by presenting your offer more specifically. Test multiple different offers and incentives before finally settling down on one.

Things To Remember

The biggest obstacle in buying something is the fear of buying something useless and thus wasting your money and looking stupid.

You eliminate this fear by giving your customers a risk free deal and thus making it easier for them to take action.

Your risk free offer should be clearly displayed in all your marketing campaigns.

Make your offer more effective by not only promising to refund the money but at the same time paying an incentive as compensation.

Make your offer very specific and detailed. Clear specific offers outperform vague offers.

To make your offer better than your competitors, either offer more compensation or more time period or make your offer more specific and detailed.

FIVE: TARGET THE RIGHT PEOPLE

"Know your target audience. Always keep them at the forefront of your mind. Understand their lifestyle and what they are looking for. Gather their feedback and use it to tailor your approach. The voice of the consumer is an essential input into the development of any fashion business or blog." – Imran Amed

It takes a lot of time, money and resources to get someone to trust you enough to buy from you. You can't afford to spend all that time and resources on people who are not interested in your products or who just can't afford them.

You should only get people who are seriously interested in your offer and has the power to make the decision of purchasing it.

Don't run after the quantity, run after quality. Put your time and effort into getting right people not more people.

You're wasting a lot of time and resources if you don't clearly understand who your targets are and go after every suspect.

Instead of running after suspects, go after prospects.

Suspects are the people who probably somehow someway in the future might be interested in your offer or be able to afford it.

Prospects are people who are ready and capable of buying your product right now. They are interested in your offer and have the power and capability to purchase it right now.

All the ads and marketing material you put out must contain very specific and clear details on what result your product delivers and how much money it costs, so that only the right prospects respond to your ad.

For example: a real estate agent shouldn't run an ad saying how great he is. The ad should be like, "Want a 2 bedroom apartment in Beverly Hills, California? Price starting from $500K, Contact me…"

The ad example above only attracts people who want a condo in Beverly Hills, CA and have 500k or more to invest. They are the right prospects (in this case).

Targeting the people that are most likely to do business with you and focusing all your time and efforts into marketing only to them, would increase your output while at the same time reduce your work.

You would start earning more money while working for less time.

Finding Prospects

Define to yourself who your target prospects are in as much details as you possibly could. Ask yourself, what people are most likely to buy your products or services?

Then figure out where those people are and how can you reach them. What magazines do they read? Where do they hang out? What TV show do they watch? What seminars or events do they attend? Where do they live? Etc.

Put your advertisement on those places. A banner ad in that magazine or newspaper, a video ad in the break of that TV show, a billboard ad in that locality etc.

Make your advertisement as specific towards those people as possible so that only they find it appealing and only they approach you or your company. Design it in such a way that the ad itself filter out non-targeted people.

For example; if you sell a high end product, make the people who're interested in buying it, first buy a small book or video demonstrating your product before reaching out to you. This way they will have to spend money and only people who are seriously interested in the product would spend any money.

Another method to find highly qualifying prospects is by renting the mailing list of people who are most likely to buy your product or service.

You can rent mailing lists based upon customer's Job, Locality, Business, Income Level, Number of members in family, Health issues, previously bought items, and on and on and on.

For example: You can rent the mailing list of people who've previously bought a certain product that goes along with what you offer, this way you know those people need your product and therefore are more likely to buy it.

You can rent lists based upon many more categories such as: voters, donors, Christians, Muslims, 20-30 years old, 30-40 years old, dog owners, swimming pool owners, people with debt, and hundreds of thousands of other categories.

The people who are not interested in what you're offering are not going to buy it, no matter how persuasive your ads are. Therefore find people, who have previously bought products similar to yours, they are sure to be interested in your products.

Other people about whom you can be sure are interested in your products are; People who have previously attended some seminar related to the topic of your product, people who have bought some book or course related to your product's topic, people who have bought another product similar to yours or that goes along with yours, people who are members of a specific group or organization that relates with your product's topic.

To get the list of such people, go to the magazine associations that relate with the topic of your business and rent all of their customers or subscriber's names and addresses.

For example; if you're an real estate agent then rent the lists of subscribers to real estate magazines, investment magazines etc.

Figure out what other businesses or industries have the customers that you want? Approach those businesses and make a deal with them in exchange for the details of their customers.

In exchange you can offer to give them; a one-time fixed amount of money, constant monthly or yearly recurring payments, a part of the profit that you generate from the people of their list or the availability of your customer list to them (since you both deals with the same type of customers, you can exchange your lists and both sides can profit).

Also, go to your direct competitors and ask them for the list of their non-converted people (people whom they tried to sell but failed). In exchange, offer to give them a part of the profit that you make (if you made any) from the people of their list.

Your Customer List

Your own customer list could be a powerful source of additional income for your business. Just like you want the customer list of other businesses, there are hundreds (if not thousands) of other businesses that would be interested in your customer list and would pay a good amount of money to rent it.

To build your own customer list do this; every time some new person indulges in a business transaction with you, ask them for their name, address, city, state, zip code and phone number.

Tell your customers they will receive mails about new offers, deals, discounts, coupons and other business related announcements.

If you don't want to ask them personally, you can have forms printed out with these questions and can ask every customer to fill out the form.

In exchange you can instantly give them a small but useful gift for free or you can give them a discount on whatever product they've just bought from you.

This list would help you identify all your active and inactive customers and stay in touch with them.

Frequently contact them through mail, and offer them great deals, discounts and rewards for doing business with you.

Divide the customers of your list according to their purchasing habits. Create different segments for different type of customers for example; regular customers, occasional or irregular customers, larger unit buying customers, inactive customers etc.

Send the details of this list to all the list brokers you know and let them rent your list to other businesses. The brokers would take the orders, deliver the list and collect payment and would send you money after cutting their 20% commission.

Most of the lists are rented for "one-time-use" only. Most businesses initially rent 5,000-10,000 names and test their results. If businesses earn profit marketing to the list, only then they rent again.

This isn't going to be a big source of income for you, at the very best you can earn a couple thousand dollars per year by renting out your customer list, but the income would be passive and automatic.

Things To Remember

Don't run after quantity instead run after quality.

Don't find suspects, find prospects.

Suspects are people who might someday in future buy your product.

Prospects are people who want or need your product right now and have the power and capability to pay for it.

Design your ads in a way that they themselves eliminate all the suspects and only attract prospects to you.

Figure out who your target prospects are? Where you can find them? And How you ca reach them?

Rent customer lists of other businesses that have your target prospects in them.

Create an additional passive income source for yourself by renting out your customer list to other businesses.

Conclusion

"Knowing is not enough, we must apply. Willing is not enough we must do" – Bruce Lee

The strategies you read above works. They work for every business in every industry. They work offline, they work online, they work for legal businesses and even for illegal businesses. They always work.

Every single strategy has the power and capability of boosting your business but I suggest that to get best results, you use them in combination with each other.

Test them on a small scale first, there's nothing you can lose anyways. When you see them work and begin to believe them, then apply them on large scale.

Look for marketing strategies used by other big and successful businesses. Observe how they get their clients and how they sell to them. Every time you see such an example ask yourself, can this method be used in my business?

Keep a notebook with you at all time or have a note keeping app in your phone, whenever and wherever you find an ad or marketing method being practiced that gets your attention and interest, write it down in your notebook or click a picture of that ad. Learn from it and apply similar technique in your business.

These strategies always work, there's no doubt about that, they are guaranteed to grow your business and increase your earnings. Just put in the work.

Get ready for more customers and more money while working with integrity and living a great life.